Courage Over Clarity

Living boldly for Christ

Elizabeth West

BookLeaf Publishing

India | USA | UK

Made with ❤ on the BookLeaf Publishing Platform
www.bookleafpub.in
www.bookleafpub.com

Dedication

This book is dedicated to God. May all I do bring glory to You.

Preface

Creativity feels like a massage for the brain. Finding
rhythmic or flowing ways to express deep thoughts and
inner feelings, feels like satisfying an itch. I hope these
poems are entertaining to read, and that some strike a
cord, or provoke deeper thought or considerations for
those who take the time to read them.

Acknowledgements

I would like to acknowledge my mom, Becky Hart, who showed me what it means to be capable. She also taught me to love and respect God, and be compassionate to others. She is the toughest and kindest person I know!

1. Courage Before Clarity

What is faith?

Faith is trust in God,

hope in the unseen.

Faith is silence,

silence to hear all that God is saying.

Faith is doing,

doing what He said.

Faith is moving,

moving forward without dread.

Faith is pushing fear away,

marching forward without delay.

Faith is not about having all the answers

or knowing how it will be done;

But faith is fully trusting in the Father

while being guided by the son.

Faith is standing up and taking action,

no longer a slave to sin.

Faith is pushing out the darkness

to allow more light within.

Faith is in the heart,

which drives the body forward.

Faith is just the start,

the first step to an eternal reward.

Sometimes it will take courage

before the clarity.
Sometimes you've just got to start moving,
and only then might you see.
Sometimes you may never know
during this life, the plan;
But always your God is for you,
so with Him you should stand.

2. Heart Tablets

The word is alive.
It is a breathing thing.
When one reads it,
forever they are changed.
The more one absorbs it,
the more it soaks within.
The more one learns it,
the more they repel sin.
The word should go with us,
wherever we may roam.
It's easy to carry it with us,
when our hearts are made it's home.
The Apostles did not have a new Bible
to hold in their hand.
They had the words of Jesus,
they passed verbally all across the land.
Mary didn't have the New Testament
with its print denoted red.
But she cherished each work and deed,
and every word Christ said.
The books were not yet printed,
they had no tablets of stone.
The had yet to start the writing,
yet they could feel it in their bones.

All those who had met with Jesus,
or been touched by Him in some way,
felt his presence in their life,
no doubt, since that day.
We can still feel it now,
just as they did from the start.
As long as we have
His words written in our heart.

3. Prayer for Intercession

Lord I prayed for intercession,
for Your will to be done.
I prayed for Your protection,
Father, Holy Ghost, and Son.
I prayed for Your redemption,
the sins no longer to bare.
I prayed for Your conviction,
as that seemed but only fair.
I prayed for Your saving grace,
because I know your love is true.
I prayed all this in Your name,
because I knew You would come through.
I fasted as I prayed,
believing all was well.
I trusted and gave gratitude,
just waiting for time to tell.
My waiting wasn't long,
for just the very next day,
my prayers were answered in the most precious way.

4. Protect Me from Me

Lord God You are amazing,
Your ways are beyond understanding.
You hear my prayers
You see my needs
You guide my path
You set me free.
Your ways are above my ways
Your timing is more than divine.
You've set Your hand upon me
I've seen Your miraculous signs.
I've prayed for my protection,
from all the dangers that abound.
I've asked for you to go before me,
to make my footing sound.
You've watched my every step,
and kept me safe as I go.
You've kept dangers away,
or helped the way forward to show.
But more than any other thing,
there is the truth I see.
With all the things you've guarded me from,
the biggest has been from me.

5. Through Him

Through Him alone,
my worth is made known.
Through His sacrifice,
when He gave His life.
Through His blood that was spilled,
Could my life's purpose be filled.
Through His death on that cross,
and the mourning and loss.
Through the persecution and pain,
came resurrection and gain.
Through Christ alone,
the way was bought,
the battle won,
and death was defeated,
placing Christ on the throne.

6. Breath

Each breath a gift.
Each breath a weapon,
if not harnessed.
Each breath a skill,
a thing to master,
a meditation,
a reprieve,
a centering and cleansing act.
We breath to live,
We breath to fight,
We breath to think,
and do what's right.

7. Mates

God gave us this blessing,
endearing to our hearts.
A partner so refreshing,
reviving broken parts.
A union full of blessings,
enriching to the core.
A love so enduring,
meant to last forevermore.
But love everlasting,
must always be adored.
Cherish every moment,
as that's what brings forth more.

8. Use Your Resources

The war is raging around you,
thoughts try to flood your mind.
Negativity tries to defeat you,
convincing you that you are in a bind.
The thoughts, they spiral,
telling you how bad you are.
But God gave you dominion over them,
so put those thoughts in a jar.
Take every thought into captivity,
so obedience to Christ may prevail.
Armored in the word of God,
cast those demons back to Hell.

(2 Corinthians 10:5)

9. Speak Life

The Bible tells us that death and life are in the power of
the tongue (Proverbs 18:20-21).
And he who prophesies speaks edification and
exhortation and comfort to men (1 Corinthians 14:3).
Your idle words will be judged (Matthew 12:36)
but no man can control his tongue (James 3).
So we must trust God to let the words of our mouth
and meditations of our heart to be acceptable in His sight
(Psalm 19:14).
Avoiding, as much as it depends on us, gossip, idle
chatter, lies, exaggeration,
harsh attack, and uncharitable remarks (Proverbs 12:22).
Speak life unto others, not hurtful or harsh words
(Ephesians 4:29).
God's word is sharper than any two-edge sword
(Hebrews 4:12),
and is much more proficient and capable of cutting away
evil than stabbing words (Psalm 75:10).
The word of God is alive, (Isaiah 55:11)
and there for your teaching and reproof (2 Timothy 3:16-
17).
Use it!

10. Your Deeds Will Be Judged

In the end,
all your deeds will be judged,
for worse or for better.
All that you do,
will be weighed unto you.
The books opened up,
each deed weighed, written, seen, known.
All those who didn't confess to Jesus Christ and His
holiness,
will be drawn up from their depth,
rank ordered by their lies and hurt,
harm and deceit,
then thrown back down into that burning lake in eternal
defeat.
But those who chose their Savior's path,
rejoice with their God,
by his side,
with peace that will ever last.

11. Brave Little Bird

As I sit, look and see,
all that is of God's great glory.
The trees as they sway,
and the lake as it flows.
The blue clear sky,
and the rocky shore below.
A brave little bird,
took it as a test.
Seeing the crumbs at my feet,
thinking only of the taste so sweet.
Took the risk as it inched closer,
to snag a morsel,
then fly back to his nest.

12. Camping

The peace that flows through my bones
when I'm outside,
our family together,
all alone.
Peace like a river,
or the lake at dawn.
Peace so pure,
clean air in my lungs.
Happiness it bubbles to the surface with a smile,
and a laugh on my tongue.
The simple joy and pleasure that come,
held forever in my heart,
until my living is done.

13. Anniversary

Celebrations, true elations,
congratulations, adorations.
A time spent thoughtfully in consideration
of how it all came to be.
So much building, so much coaxing,
so much love, so much romance.
So much hard times, and so much stress.
But nonetheless,
all these times brought us from point A to point B.
And next year this time,
we will be celebrating making it to point C.
Together through this journey of life,
I'm thankful to celebrate
being your wife.

14. Pleasure in Waiting

Giving of yourself
in such an intimate way
should be savored,
as breaths are labored,
feelings that have been growing,
day by day.
Passion so intense,
sensations so true,
release so fulfilling,
this gift from God for just you two.
So much pleasure,
daily getting better,
the love you'll be making,
the reward unfailing,
your treasure for waiting,
connected forever
through the vows of love.

15. Death

Death
A word with such negative connotations.
It incurs thoughts of black emptiness,
sadness, gloom.
Knock on wood,
spit in your hat.
Heart starts racing
to prove it hasn't got you, yet.
Heavy breaths,
and saddened eyes,
as if those who are dead,
are the losers of life.
As if death is something
that can somehow be avoided.
As if it's the worst thing
anyone could imagine.
But what is death
but a transition.
A brief interlude
between one life and the next.
Death is but an instant,
fleeting as quickly as it comes.
Death is nothing more,
than a door.

Without Christ,
it's the destination
that should be feared much more.

16. Your Riches Will Rot

How deceptive wealth can be,
Thinking it's the answer
that will set you free.
How corrosive the snare
of silver and gold.
That once captures you,
strengthens it's hold.
How difficult it is to escape
fancy garments sealing your fate.
How lonely it will be
when in death
it all rots with thee.

17. Rivers of Water

Always flowing,
never ending,
rivers of water run.
Passing by,
washing over,
through the valleys,
glinting sun.
Rivers of water,
full of life.
Refreshing, renewing, resounding springs.
One of life's most marvelous things.
Never ending,
Never ceasing,
forever changing,
changing me.
Holy Spirit
pouring forth,
as fast and renewing
as rivers of water run.

18. Thief

The Devil is a sly old fox,
his trickery is uncanny.
You think you are doing things of worth,
all the while you are really just panning.
The time you spend is quickly gone,
wasted moments, unending Toks,
minutes turned into hours.
Lost moments, days, and years,
until at last the end is here.
And then too late to save your fate,
from a life that was lived unfulfiled.

19. In-Dependence

I can do this,
I can cover that.
I can do it all with the sweat of my back.
Pressing harder, moving further.
Striving day and night.
Moving faster, never backwards,
forging the way I call right.
Finally finished,
hunched and twisted,
yet nothing here to show.
If only I'd listened,
traded in some independence,
perhaps I could have watched the flowers grow.

(Exodus 16:18)

20. Listen

How loud is the voice of God,
with thunder to His words.
How clear are His commands,
so easily to be observed.
How mighty is His tone,
that directs us to His mission.
The only trouble is when
you forget to listen.

21. The Sound of a Sunrise

What sound does a sunrise make,
as it's lifting from the earth?
What sound is at dawn's break,
as the wind sweeps in from the south?
The sound of waking trees and dew covered grass,
lifting forth to meet the sun as it slowly moves past.
What sound does the moon make,
as it bows down beneath the earth?
What sound does the dusk make,
as it fades out at last?
The sound of light and shadows,
fighting for fights sake.
The sound of new beginnings,
falling into place.

22. Your Miracles Still Abound

Thank you Jesus for Your works,
so many have You done.
I see Your love daily,
and as surely as the sun.
You have blessed me in oh so many ways,
Your protection covering me.
You have seen me through so many days,
so many blessings to be seen.
You do things both small and great,
to show your children love.
You washed away so many mistakes,
raining grace from above.
Money you have blessed me with,
in just the nick of time.
Healing has swept in miraculously,
and You've protected me from crime.
Relationships recovered,
 in the blink of an eye.
Resolutions discovered,
just beyond a good cry.
But now you are just showing off,
I know this is true,

because not only did you heal my sight,
you also manifested a missing shoe!

23. Do the Hard Things

When life gets hectic,
and everything seems hard.
When life's a challenge,
and your brain feels jarred.
Keep fighting the battle,
keep pushing forward.
Keep getting back on the saddle,
and just keep praising the Lord.
Your God is mighty,
and has power in his veins.
Your God can help you,
His spirit remains.
He will help you fight your battle,
with you only needing to be still.
Keep fighting the battles,
and doing His will.
The Lord is your comfort,
in times when things are rough.
He's got you covered,
His love is enough.
Keep fighting the battles,
and doing the hard things.
He'll bless you and keep you,
through anything.

24. The Woman Who Cried

How great the power
of the Lord on high,
how amazing is his grace.
He is always by our side,
shining down his loving face.
How beautifully,
He tenderly cares.
How magnificently,
our sins He does bare.
Could you imagine,
feeling His love,
and knowing He came
from the Father above?
Could you imagine,
meeting Him there?
Lounging at table,
as you washed His feet with your hair?
How it must have felt,
knowing the weight of her sin,
feeling it lifted,
filled with peace all within.
The sense of complete ease,
washing away all the hurts from her past.
She was renewed,

she felt salvation at last.
Could you imagine,
your heart open wide,
washing your Savior's feet as you began to cry?
Singing Hallelujah,
your joy would proclaim.
There's something so precious,
in just calling His name.

25. Healing

Healing isn't about worth,
as the woman who touches Christ's hem.
Healing isn't about having it all together,
ask the man they called Legion.
Healing isn't about location,
ask the son of the Centurion.
Healing isn't about denomination,
ask the Romans and Samaritans.
Healing comes from believing,
and being vulnerable enough to ask.
Healing comes from perceiving,
knowing he's up for the task.
Healing comes from knowing,
just what the Lord can do.
And putting your faith in Jesus,
to help see you through.
Sometimes the healing comes from
our faith and trust alone.
Sometimes it comes from the faith of others,
when our hearts are more like stone.
Faith and intercession,
and people agreeing in prayers for you.
When two or more are gathered,
there is no limit to what God can do.

26. Trials and Tribulations

Trials and tribulations
will tempt you to go astray.
Trials and tribulations
will test you in every way.
Trails will have you thinking
what is the point in all of this.
They will cause your faith to start shrinking,
they will steal your sense of bliss.
Tribulations will hit you hard
and take your breath away.
They will find ways to distract you,
then can easily cause you to stray.
Our thoughts will often get selfish,
our pride gets in our own way.
But all this can be avoided,
if you just stay in the Word and pray.

27. Holding Pattern

Are you stuck in a holding pattern?
Going in circles but not getting anywhere?
Do you feel like you are wasting time?
Feeling like your moving,
but stopped on a dime?
It's easy to get stuck in a hold.
Doing the same ol' things,
but recognizing it's getting old.
Sometimes these holds come from inside.
Getting caught in the motions of the day to day stride.
Sometimes the holds come from some place greater.
God's got good plans,
and He's not a traitor.
Sometimes the hold is setting things in motion.
You just need to remember,
His love is wider than the ocean.

28. Ask/Recieve

Those who ask, will receive.
Those with faith, those who believe.
Our Father in Heaven, He loves us so.
He wants what is best for us,
He wants to help us grow.
Jesus told the story of the son who ran away.
How happy was his father when no longer did he stray.
He didn't but barely ask,
and his father quickly came through.
He didn't merely fulfill his request,
but far greater did he do.
This same way our Lord and Savior will also prove true.
Jesus says it over and over again,
during his sermon on the mound.
Don't fret, but only ask, and the answer will be found.
Don't stress, but only request,
holding faith in what is true.
And Jesus our Good Lord is more than happy
to do it for you.
The only thing He says you'll need,
Is faith the size of a mustard seed.

29. Faith/Family/Connection

God created us in the likeness of Him.
God created family in the likeness of them.
Father, Son, and Holy Spirit,
three in one.
Not a single entity,
but a Trinity that won't be undone.
The Father didn't create us
so that we should be alone.
But he gave us all a family,
to guide us until we reach home.
Family can be a simple one,
of mother, brother, dad.
But often it consists even more
of the friends we have and had.
Our circle is a growing one,
made from love inside.
Encompassing others who surround us,
if we dare not to run and hide.
Our family keeps us grounded,
and helps light our path on through.
This tiring path we walk while
striving to stay true.
We know this world is not our home,
we are sojourners on this journey.

And as long as we walk in the light we will get there.
No need to be in a hurry.
So keep your family close,
and love one another with all your might.
God gave us each a family,
so we ought to treat them right.

30. Be Grateful

There is so very much to be grateful for.
Everthything from feeling the love of the Father,
to the absence of war.
We are so very lucky,
more than I ever could express.
When we look at just how lucky we are,
we see there is just no need to be stressed.
We have so much food to eat,
never have I suffered.
We have so much water to drink,
my lips have yet to sputter.
My clothes all fit and none have holes.
My shoes are shiny and white,
without worry of threadbare soles.
Getting to work and school is such a delight,
riding in the air conditioning,
while listening to Touch the Sky.
Just having access to school for my children alone,
is quite the blessing.
There's so much we take advantage of,
as if life were depressing.
We forget to open up our eyes
to all the good around.
We act sometimes as if our while world

is set on shaky ground.
If we only would take a moment
and truly contemplate,
we would so quickly find there is so much in every day
 for us to appreciate.
The sun shining bright,
the birds of a feather,
the love of our friends,
life is just getting better!

www.ingramcontent.com/pod-product-compliance
Lightning Source LLC
Chambersburg PA
CBHW050950030426
42339CB00007B/368